AF572076

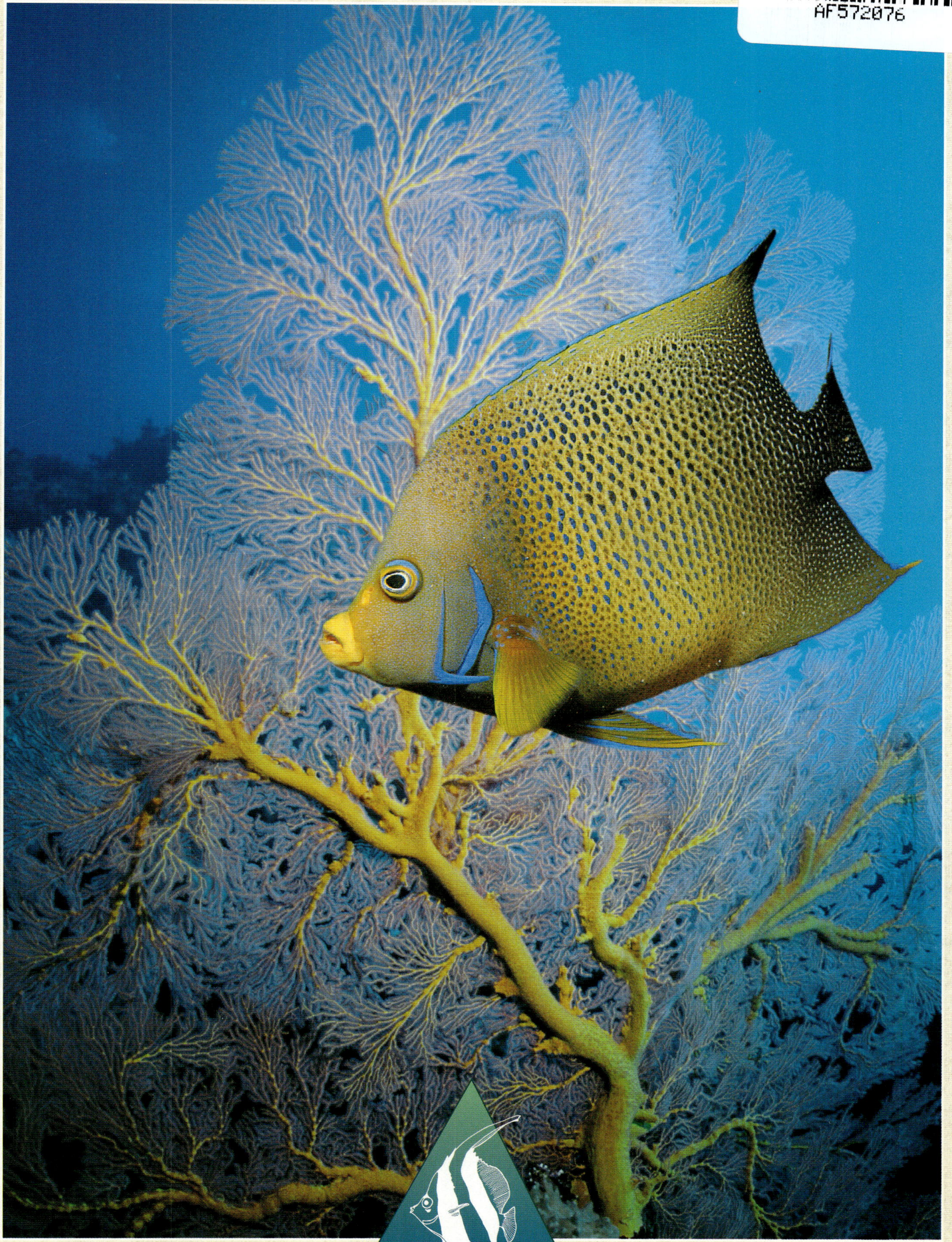

QUEENSLAND

AUSTRALIA

Left: The sailing ship "America" went aground on the reef flat at Wreck Island in 1831
Left inset and above: Aspects of the Reef

WHEN IT ALL BEGAN

The tiny animals whose limestone skeletons form coral reefs first appeared in the world's seas over 500 million years ago. The northern part of the Great Barrier Reef was established around 18 million years ago, while the southern part dates to only two million years before the present. Variations in sealevel have killed many successive reefs, and today's Great Barrier Reef had its origins around 6000 years ago.

Sunshine Coral

Lady Musgrave Island is at the western end of a large lagoon

Coral debris on Lady Elliot Island

A coral cay is formed from coral debris broken from a reef

The Low Isles are offshore from Port Douglas

THE BIRTH OF A CORAL CAY

Coral reefs are built by countless tiny, soft-bodied polyps, which extract minerals from the seawater and use them to construct their homes. A founder polyp will divide to create a colony of minute, tentacled creatures encased in limestone exoskeletons. Corals which live in warm tropical seas host in their tissues minute plants called zooxanthellae, which use energy from sunlight and boost the coral's limestone-forming capacity. Algae and other materials cement coral colonies together to form reefs.

As parts of a reef are broken away, waves deposit the debris and high tides build up the deposit until it breaks the surface. Water acting on cay sediments forms protective beachrock. Birds and other animals arrive, nutrients accumulate in the sand and plants take root. Eventually, a coral cay has formed.

Main picture: Green Island is a 13-hectare coral cay off Cairns
Above inset left to right: Pioneer beach grasses send runners over the sand; Pandanus is also called the Screw Palm; colonies of birds like these Crested Terns fertilise coral cays

Above: Pisonia trees have sticky seeds, often dispersed by nesting birds
Above inset left to right: Coastal Sheoaks may grow close to the beach; Crested Terns nest on coral cays; Pandanus grows near the shoreline

STARTING FROM SCRATCH

Unlike continental islands, which were cut off from the mainland with cargoes of plants and animals, coral cays are sterile environments. The plant seeds carried onto the cay by the wind, by the ocean, or by birds must establish themselves in coral sand which is gradually enriched by nutrients from bird guano and from decaying plants and animals. Success leads to success, for once plants grow, more birds are attracted to the cay and the cycle of life continues.

Crested Terns rest on a wreck

A Red-tailed Tropicbird feeds its downy chick

WINGS OVER THE REEF

Even the most desolate of the Reef's coral cays, its gleaming sand and grey-white coral rubble bare of vegetation, serves as a resting place and possible breeding ground for birds such as terns, gulls and gannets. As greenery takes root, they will be joined by shearwaters, noddies, frigatebirds and tropicbirds. The reef flats and beaches will attract herons and waders, while, in time, doves, rails and white-eyes will fly in and make the island their home. Heat, the vagaries of tropical weather and predation mean that many chicks do not reach maturity. Colonial nesters such as terns are especially vulnerable to disturbance, for once a guarding parent leaves eggs or small chicks they fall prey to predatory gulls. Gannets and boobies are preyed-upon by the Reef's magnificent pirates, the frigatebirds, which engage in aerial thuggery to force their victims to disgorge the fish they are carrying islandwards for their chicks.

A Masked Gannet feeds fish to its fledgling

A pair of Brown Boobies

Brown Noddy and chick

White-capped Noddies on their nest

Female Great Frigatebird

Pair of Crested Terns

Red-footed Booby

Top left and clockwise: Wings over the Reef: Black-naped Tern; Great Frigatebird; Bridled Tern; Roseate Tern

Above: The Red-tailed Tropicbird, one of the Reef's most spectacular species

LAGOONS AND REEF FLATS

The Great Barrier Reef covers over 230,000 square kilometres and contains many different sorts of reef.

The coral formations most often seen by visitors to the Great Barrier Reef are fringing reefs, formed along the edge of the mainland, or ringing continental islands. Further north are barrier reefs, rooted on land which is sinking so slowly that coral polyps can build upwards to keep pace with its subsidence. Deeper water between reef and land, or between cay and reef flat, is known as a lagoon.

A coral reef is constantly battered and broken up by waves. Marine creatures also take their toll: worms bore through the coral, fish rasp and chomp away at it in search of algae, molluscs carve homes in it. Shells and the skeletons of tiny single-celled animals join the coral chunks and sand rolled along by the water. They are finally deposited where water flow slows, the heavier pieces on the windward side of a forming cay and the smaller pieces and sand on the leeward side, where they spread out to form a reef flat.

Reef flats and coral cays

Main picture: Reef-building corals grow best where sunlight can reach their "solar cells", the zooxanthellae
Inset left to right: Exploring the reef flat

Top: Underwater photography captures lifetime memories of the Reef
Above: Juvenile Convictfish and surgeonfish in a lagoon
Opposite: These explorers are taking care not to damage fragile reef life
Opposite inset above and below: Life in the lagoon

Top: Drummer Fish and Sergeant Majors
Above: On one or two nights each year, each coral polyp releases eggs and sperm into the water. Fertilised eggs become planulae, which settle, change into polyps and found new colonies. These enlarge by each polyp dividing into two individuals

The Hawksbill's mottled shell was used for "tortoiseshell" ornaments

The Loggerhead nests on Wreck Island and at Mon Repos, near Bundaberg

The Leatherback, which may weigh up to 500 kg, swims long distances from temperate feeding grounds to tropical breeding grounds

The Flatback Turtle is unique to Australia and has a flattened shell covered by a thin skin

The Olive Ridley is the smallest of the world's sea turtles

Flatback and Loggerhead, like all sea turtles, cry "tears" which excrete the salt swallowed with seawater

SEA TURTLES

Six of the world's seven species of sea turtles live and nest along the Great Barrier Reef. In the past fifty years, numbers of sea turtles have declined so much world-wide that five species are considered to be endangered. The Queensland coast is one of the few places where these fascinating reptiles can still be seen in numbers.

Several areas where female sea turtles come ashore to lay their eggs are easily reached by visitors to the Reef. The best time for viewing is between November and February, when tides are high between 8 pm and midnight. A female drags herself up the beach, digs a body pit at the bottom of which she scoops an egg chamber, then lays her leathery eggs. The egg chamber and body pit are filled with sand, then the female laboriously lumbers down the beach to the water. The warm sand incubates the eggs, and hatchlings emerge from January to April. Only one in 1000 may survive to mature 40 or more years later.

Loggerhead female laying in her egg chamber

Loggerhead hatchling

Flatback hatchling

Top: *Green Turtle female laying eggs*
Above: *Returning to the sea after egg-laying*
Left: *Green Turtle underwater*

ABOUT THE GREEN TURTLE

The Green Turtle is the most common nesting species on southern Great Barrier Reef islands. The Green Turtle feeds entirely on seaweeds and seagrasses. This makes its flesh very palatable and humans have traditionally hunted adult Green Turtles and taken their eggs.

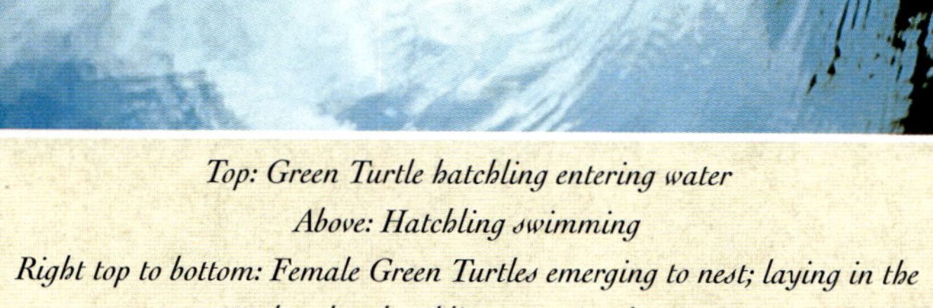

Top: Green Turtle hatchling entering water
Above: Hatchling swimming
Right top to bottom: Female Green Turtles emerging to nest; laying in the egg-chamber; hatchling emerging from egg

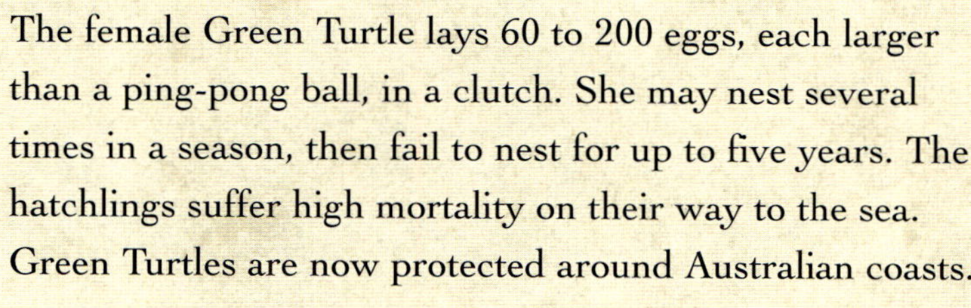

The female Green Turtle lays 60 to 200 eggs, each larger than a ping-pong ball, in a clutch. She may nest several times in a season, then fail to nest for up to five years. The hatchlings suffer high mortality on their way to the sea. Green Turtles are now protected around Australian coasts.

Above: A magnificent featherstar
Below: the Trumpet Fish sucks in prey with its tubelike mouth

BIZARRE REEF CREATURES

The Reef is home to many marine animals which appear strange but are perfectly adapted to their environment. There is a lifeform to exploit every ecological niche. While many seemingly odd creatures are harmless to humans, others should be admired from a safe distance.

The Leaf Scorpion Fish (above) and the Lionfish (left) are members of a family of fishes whose spines may be coated with toxic mucus

Coral Trout

A MULTICOLOURED JIGSAW

There are over 1500 species of fish recorded from the Great Barrier Reef so far, and more waiting to be discovered. Up to 860 different species have been found on a single reef.

From the open sea, and the steep slopes where corals drop to the ocean bed, across the reef crest to the sheltered lagoon and reef flat, there are refuges and feeding grounds for fish of all shapes and most sizes and a bewildering and dazzling array of colours. Each species has its preferred habitat for feeding and resting. These fish-favoured niches interlock and overlap to form an intricate Reef jigsaw puzzle. Studying the behaviour patterns of any of these fish is a fascinating and relaxing occupation.

Soft and Gorgonian Corals provide fish habitats

Opposite top: Juvenile Sea Perch

Featherstars, Gorgonian Coral and hard coral

Bannerfish and Coral Cod

Squirrelfish and Royal Angelfish

Blenny hiding in coral

Damselfish take refuge in a coral fortress

FORTRESSES OF CORAL

"Hard" corals are the stony limestone homes protecting the fragile bodies of around 350 different species of coral polyps. There are fewer species of "soft" corals, whose colonies are either supported by needles of limestone in the polyps' flesh, or, like the gorgonians, have horny skeletons.

The shape of a coral colony depends upon its species and also upon the influences of waves, currents and exposure at low tide. Where the light level is low, corals grow in large plates, so their zooxanthellae get maximum exposure to the sun. Where wave action is vigorous, the corals are short, stubby and strong. Coral on the highest part of a reef may take the form of smooth sheets offering little resistance to the flow of water as tides ebb and flow.

At night, when the polyps expand to feed, coral flowers in many colours, the hues largely determined by the pigmentation of the zooxanthellae in their tissues. During the day, many corals appear drab, for the polyps are withdrawn. However, species of fish whose hues become subdued as they sleep amongst the coral at night show brilliant colours during day.

Each coral formation has its resident fish, swimming in and out of crevices, taking refuge under ledges, poking in debris for food. Isolated "bommies" of coral may be particularly rich in life, focuses for schools of jewel-coloured small fish and, where they are not harassed, for much larger individuals.

Coral and fish abound at Fitzroy Island

Opposite: Moses Perch shelter under ledges of Plate Coral on the reef slope

Mushroom Coral (above) and Slipper Coral

Featherstars are protected between fingerlike hard corals

The tentacles of coral polyps, armed with stinging cells, capture minute animals

There is great diversity of coral patterns

Vase Coral

Coral colonies form a living mosaic

Staghorn Coral

Blue Tang in branching coral

Above: Soft corals

SOFT CORALS, FANS AND WHIPS

The white limestone skeletons of hard corals create reefs. Soft corals are leathery in texture, may be dramatically coloured and are supported by tiny internal crystal structures called sclerites. Some soft corals can change size and shape by retracting their polyps. The group of gorgonian corals includes the sea fans and whips, most of which have flexible skeletons. Many extend nets and meshes bearing polyps which efficiently sieve potential food from the water. Soft and hard corals and gorgonians belong to a group called coelenterates, which also includes the floating sea jellies and less mobile sea anemones.

A soft coral shelters a commensal brittle star

Opposite: This soft coral has spines to protect its polyps against predators

Orange-fin Anemone Fish and their host anemone

This Porcelain Crab also shelters in an anemone

LIVING TOGETHER

The tentacles of anemones bear lethal stinging cells. An anemone fish takes refuge inside an anemone after a period of repeated brief visits, which enable the fish to build up a protective coating of mucus from the tentacles. All anemone fish begin life as male. A typical group contains a large female, a smaller, mature male and immature males. If the female disappears, the mature male changes sex and an immature male takes over his role. Nesting anemone fish nip at a spot on the base of their anemone so it pulls back, then lay on the site exposed. The eggs are protected by the anemone's presence.

Opposite: At night, the anemone closes, and enfolds the anemone fish

Cleaner Wrasse removing parasites from gillcovers of a Barramundi Rock-cod

GUILDS OF CLEANERS

Fish have no hands and find it difficult to dislodge the parasites which live between their scales and inside their mouths and gillcovers. A number of fishes and shrimps, known as "cleaners", specialises in removing - and eating - these parasites.

The Cleaner Wrasse is typical of these useful operators. To advertise it is ready for business, it does a bobbing dance in the water near some landmark. Fish of all sizes, and even manta rays, come considerable distances to such a cleaning station. The wrasse then picks off parasites, dead skin and fungal growths and may even swim into the client's mouth to clean its teeth.

Above left: Cleaner Wrasse and Beaked Coralfish

Top and above inset left to right: Coral Trout at cleaning station being attended by Cleaner Wrasse: Coral Trout; wrasse entering trout's mouth; Coral Cod; Sweetlip
Right: Cleaner Wrasse and Magpie Morwong

Cleaners play a vital role in keeping fish on a reef healthy. Where cleaners are removed from a reef, the resident fish drop in numbers and those remaining become increasingly infested with parasites and fungi.

The Lionfish uses the vanes of its spectacular fins to "round up" shrimps

Bannerfish pick invertebrates from the reef

The Barramundi Rock-cod lurks awaiting prey

The Thick-lipped Wrasse is a roving invertebrate grubber

AN ABUNDANCE OF FISHES

A coral reef contains fish of an almost infinite variety of shapes and a diversity of changeable colours. They range in size from tiny gobies about 10 mm in length to enormous rays and sharks. Some of these fishes have intricate relations with particular sorts of coral or with other Reef creatures and all must find food within Reef waters.

The three main food sources for Reef fishes are the smorgasbord of minute floating plants and animals known as plankton, the algae which grow on and in coral, and other Reef animals ranging from tiny worms to fishes. Many fish have specialised ways of feeding. Some sieve through sand, others scrape algae off coral, or use powerful jaws to crush molluscs. Many are predators, lurking in ambush or pursuing prey actively through the water. Young fish are particularly vulnerable to hunters and fry of many species mass in schools for a period before the survivors seek homes around the coral.

Moses Perch

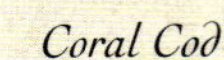

Coral Cod

Red Emperor

Teira Batfish

Eye-stripe Surgeonfish

Blue-barred Parrotfish

Harlequin Tuskfish

Dotted Sweetlip

Moorish Idol

Golden Damsel

Footballer Coral Trout

Magpie Morwong

Ring-tailed Cardinalfish

Diana's Hogfish

Tailspot Squirrelfish

Brown Anemone Fish

Half-circled Angelfish

Threadfin Butterflyfish

Highfin Coralfish

Masked Bannerfish

ANGELS, BANNERS AND BUTTERFLIES

Butterflyfish and bannerfish and their relations the angelfish are amongst the most gorgeous of the Reef's many spectacular fishes. Many species are familiar to saltwater aquarium fanciers. Butterflyfish feed on invertebrates, nipping them up from around the coral. Some species of butterflyfish even eat coral polyps, while the long beaks of other species are used forceps-fashion to tear off pieces of prey animals. Angelfish have brushlike teeth with which they scrape sponges and other organisms from the walls of coral caves and overhangs. Some species are strongly territorial and the young are often strikingly different in pattern and colour from the adults. Smaller angelfish may swim in groups consisting of a male and several females.

Blue Angelfish and Beaked Coralfish

Chevroned Butterflyfish

Emperor Angelfish

Raccoon Butterflyfish

Longfin Bannerfish

Six-banded Angelfish

Dusky Butterflyfish

Long-nosed Butterflyfish

Regal Angelfish

Humpback Whale leaping

Whaler Shark

Geoff Taylor

The harmless Whale Shark

Bigeye Trevally form dense schools

Manta Rays are plankton feeders

A school of Barracuda

PREDATORS OF THE OPEN OCEAN

The predators of the Reef and its fringing waters pursue animals which range in size from the microscopic plankton engulfed by the Humpback Whale, the Whale Shark and the Manta Ray to the larger fish and marine mammals killed or scavenged by the true sharks.

Hunters often group together and feed as co-operative units. Predatory fish, such as the Barracuda and trevallies, form schools whose numbers offer defensive protection. Such a school operates on the premise that where there is food for one, there will be food for all. The most intelligent medium-sized predators of the Reef, the dolphins, have brought co-operative pursuit of fish to a fine art.

Bottlenosed Dolphin

Above: Gold-spotted Trevally
Left: School of Golden Trevally

PELAGIC FISH

The waters off the Reef edge and the open seas beyond contain fish which feed on or near the ocean's surface. These pelagic species include marlin, sailfish, mackerel, trevally, tuna and other fish eagerly sought by sport-fishers. Unlike many of the ornate coral-reef species, pelagic fish are streamlined and sleek-scaled, able to swim fast and to make rapid changes of direction. A school of pelagic fish will turn almost in unison, shimmering and rippling to evade danger or in pursuit of food.

Schools of pelagic fish surface-feeding on small organisms become targets for fish-eating birds, such as gannets and terns and for dolphins (which may detect the presence of the school by spotting birds hovering over it).

The eggs of some reef fishes hatch into larvae which drift in the open ocean for a period which may be as long as three months. If they reach a suitable habitat, they settle and change into juvenile fish.

CUT TO CHASE

Lone human-fish,
I sink into the blue deep.
The diamond-blaze of sun behind
lights up a thousand tiny eyes ahead.
Hands outstretched, I wait to play,
but, silently a silver shape slices past me
death surfing on its fins.
Like foil shaken in moonlight
the friendly smallfry shimmer and flee,
leaving me lonely
in the indigo sea.

Blue Sea Star

Rose Sea Star

A bi-coloured feather star

Above: Ijima's Sea Urchin, tube feet extended
Left: Vermilion Biscuit Star

STARS OF THE SEA

There are five different sorts of echinoderms (spiny-skinned animals) to be found on the Reef. The sturdy sea stars and their more fragile relatives the brittle stars have five arms radiating from a central body. Sea urchins have rigid bodies, which are usually protected by bristling spines. Sea cucumbers are sausage-shaped creatures which process seabottom debris to extract food. The primitive sea lilies are represented by the lovely feather stars, which are usually seen attached to the reef, their arms extended to catch drifting plankton.

A sea cucumber
Opposite: A feather star's arms are made "feathery" by fine processes called pinnules

NOT ALL MOLLUSCS HAVE SHELLS

The Great Barrier Reef is the home of marine creatures which in the past were valued for their often beautiful shells. Today's Reef-goers realise that while shells are fascinating, the living animals which create them exhibit interesting behaviour and are often very eye-catching.

Molluscs are soft-bodied animals. Many sorts build homes of calcium carbonate into which they can retreat if threatened. The gastropod molluscs include snails and cone shells. Each gastropod creeps along on one large foot situated under its stomach, most of its body protected by its coiled shell. The striking gastropod sea slugs called nudibranchs are molluscs with no shells. Their often brilliant colours signal that they are poisonous to eat. Other molluscs, such as giant clams, have two shells and are called bivalves. Octopuses and squid are also molluscs, but are predators without protective shells, though the squid has an internal structure known as cuttlebone.

Left: Lady Musgrave Island's surrounding reef offers ideal habitat for molluscs
Inset left to right: Cowries are gastropod molluscs; a giant clam is a bivalve mollusc; this bubble shell is surrounded by a fleshy mantle

Nudibranchs may wear warning colours

Stonefish
Blue-ringed Octopus
Golden (Olive) Sea-snake
Lionfish
Stinging coral
Stinging hydroid
Sea jelly
Sea urchin
Cone shell

DANGERS OF THE REEF

Many of the Reef's animals have developed efficient ways of protecting themselves from aggressors. These mechanisms also serve to disable or kill their prey. Some species rely upon sharp teeth and powerful jaws. Sharks are not a hazard to most divers, but if seen should be treated with caution. They are scavengers and predators which may become aggressive if food seems available. Other large fish are generally friendly where not harassed or teased with food, but the good nature of species such as moray eels should not be taken for granted. Sea snakes possess powerful venom, although they are reluctant to strike unless provoked. The spectacular scorpion fish and fire fish have venomous spines on their fins, the drab stonefish has them on its back. Bottom-dwelling stingrays have venomous spines on their whiplike tails. Sea anemones have stinging tentacles, sea urchins have venom-tipped spines. The Sea Wasp (a "jellyfish"), the Blue-ringed Octopus and a number of species of cone shells also produce venom which may prove lethal to humans.

Australian Photo Library

Whaler Shark

ETIQUETTE ON THE REEF

There are two Golden Rules to be observed on the Great Barrier Reef and its islands.
The first is: LOOK BUT DO NOT TOUCH.
The second is: LEAVE THE REEF AS YOU FOUND IT.
Thoughtless behaviour or unnecessary bravado, especially underwater, can have potentially fatal consequences. Some precautions, such as wearing sunblock and donning sneakers and gloves to explore the reefs, are commonsense. Others are less obvious, for example asking local advice before eating fish (pufferfish may be toxic and some other reef species may cause ciguatera poisoning in some areas).

Is this in the best interests of either Moray Eel or human?

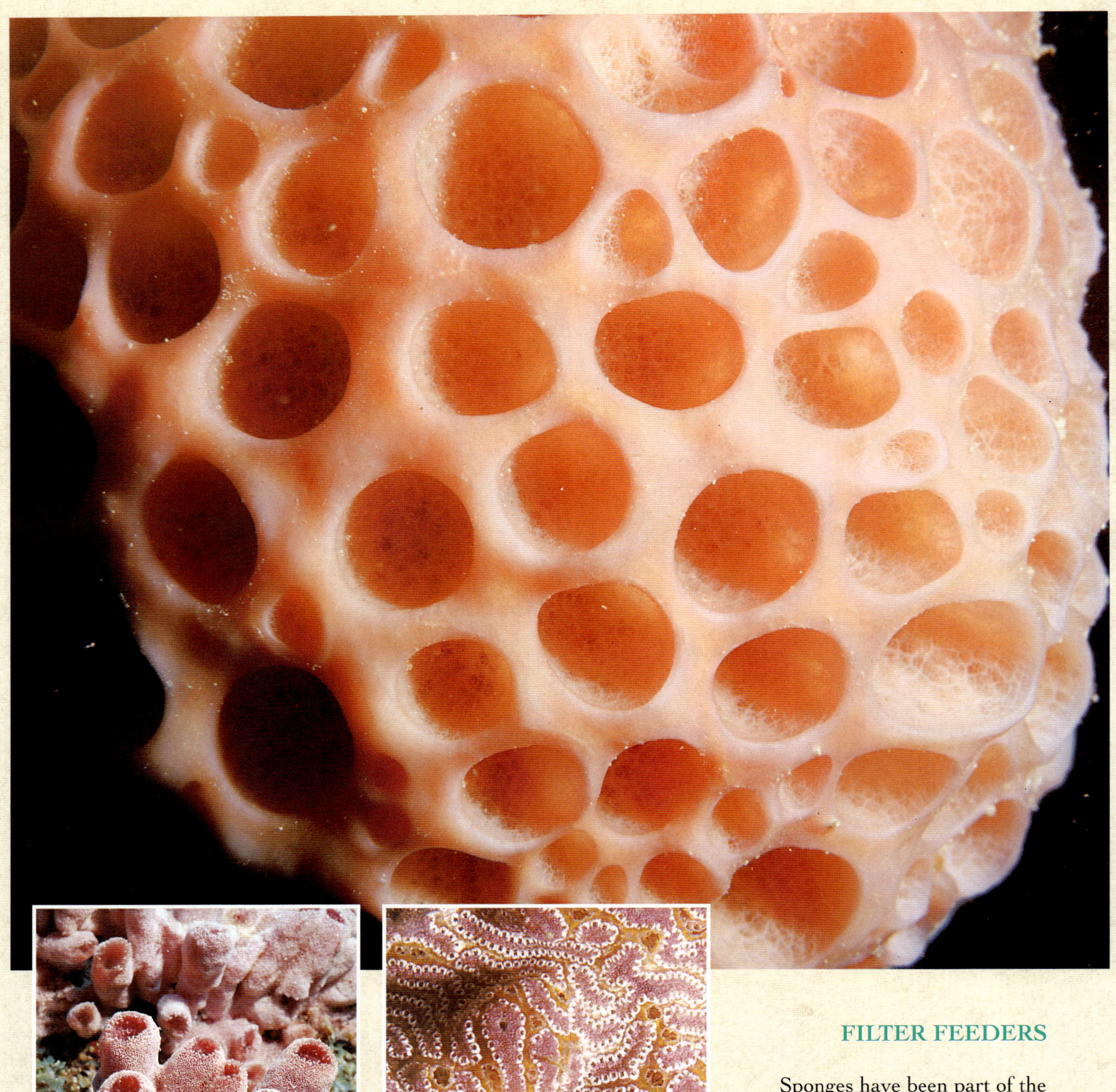

FILTER FEEDERS

Sponges have been part of the underwater world for over 60 million years. Seawater passes into a sponge through pores and is propelled through the sponge's feeding chambers by whiplike cells. Tiny particles of food are extracted, then the water is expelled through large openings. Tough-skinned ascidians, which intake water through one hole, may live singly or in colonies.

Top: A sponge has a tough skeleton covered by a thin layer of living tissue
Above left: Sponge "chimneys" increase the throughflow of water
Above right: An ascidian colony appears encrusted with jewels

Feather-duster worm

MARINE WORMS

The Reef system is full of marine worms of various kinds. Some are free-swimming, while others bore into coral or burrow into sand. The bright colours of the surface-living flatworms warn potential predators that they may be distasteful or poisonous. Many species build tube homes of varying substances. The beautiful feather-duster worms poke plumy crowns of feeding filaments from their tubes, using them to secure food drifting in the water. When a shadow falls over light-sensitive "eyes" on the crown, the vulnerable filaments are withdrawn into the tube.

These feather-duster worms have delicate, spiralling feeding filaments

Top: Painted Cray
Above inset left and right: Feeding shrimp; Shovel-nose Lobster

Coral crab

Miniature hermit crab

Above: Crab carrying eggs on its abdomen; above right: Hermit crab

CRABS AND CRAYS

A crab or a cray lives inside a suit of armour, jointed to accommodate the movement of the owner's numerous body segments. The weight of this exoskeleton is carried by the water and a cray swims forwards with the help of small swimmerets under the abdomen and backwards by flicking its powerful tail. A crab has swimmerets also, but its tail is usually folded against its abdomen and it scuttles across the reef rather than swims. The soft abdomens of hermit crabs lack armour and must be crammed into abandoned shells, discarded for larger homes as the crabs grow. Both crabs and crays use their first pairs of arms, which vary in size and are equipped with pincers, for feeding and defence. The males of some species use enlarged claws for courtship.

Banded Coral Shrimps are "cleaners" of fish

Above: Vessels relying solely on sail have always needed skilled piloting for safety in Reef waters
Photo courtesy of the Queensland Tourist and Travel Corporation

HUMANS ON THE REEF

The area upon which the present Great Barrier Reef stands was used as a place for hunting and gathering food by the Aboriginal people for tens of thousands of years. When the sea reclaimed the coastal land and today's Reef formed, the Aborigines continued their traditional way of life, using canoes to reach the islands. The first European to chart a route through the Reef was Captain James Cook, whose *Endeavour* sailed between coral and coast in 1770 and spent two months at the mouth of today's Endeavour River being repaired after striking a reef not far from Cape Tribulation. It was another English navigator, Captain Matthew Flinders, exploring the Australian coastline in the *Investigator* in 1802, who first used the term "Great Barrier Reef".

There are over one thousand nineteenth-century shipwrecks recorded from the Reef. One of the earliest wrecks, in 1791, was that of the *Pandora*, which resulted in the deaths of 31 crew and four *Bounty* mutineers. This 24-gun frigate went aground near Raine Island, on reefs which, like those of the Capricorn-Bunker Group in the south, claimed many unfortunate vessels.

All wrecks and relics within Queensland's State marine parks are protected by law and marine archaeologists have a continuing program of research at several sites.

Inset above left to right: A replica of HMS "Pandora", made by Wayne Masters of the Australian War Memorial (photo courtesy Museum of Queensland); a Reef relic; remains of gold and silver fob watch retrieved from the wreck of the "Pandora" (photo courtesy Museum of Queensland)

Convict-built tower on Raine Island

Snorkelling is a window into the Reef wonders

Scuba-diving allows deeper exploration

Fish fly above coral formations

Gorgonians and hard corals

A research station operated by the University of Sydney stands on One Tree Island

PRESERVATION OF THE REEF

The Great Barrier Reef was declared a Marine Park in 1975 and was inscribed on the World Heritage List in 1981. The Great Barrier Reef Marine Park Authority has the task of balancing the needs of an ever-increasing number of visitors, the effects of mainland industry and demands of maritime commerce with the well-being of the Reef and its plants and animals. Continuing research is vital to the future of this complex biosystem.

Opposite: Studying a sea anemone and its attendant anemone fish

Subjects for pictures are all around the photographer

CAMERAS UNDERWATER

You cannot take the Great Barrier Reef home with you, but film or videotape will help you re-create the kaleidoscopic Reef experience. The two-dimensional illusion may never fully capture the three-dimensional reality, but it will feed memory and imagination until at last you are able to return. There is no end to the complexity of the equipment available for underwater photography, but in the end it is the eye behind the camera and the instinct to capture the right scene at the crucial moment that makes great images. Simply remember that water absorbs natural colours, so the deeper you dive the bluer everything will look and electronic flash is necessary for serious work. Get the best equipment you can afford, enjoy using it and be proud of the results!

Still photographer

Taking movie film

ISLAND TIME

This is a message to all travellers
reaching safe harbour
on this wonder of the world.

Please discard your watches, stop your clocks,
put out of mind any thought of haste or hurry,
for now you are on island time.

Mark the hours by the golden glory
of sun rise, sun set.
Let the turning of the day be told
by birdshapes wheeling in from sea.
If your rhythms have to have a measure,
match them with eternal surge of ocean.

Wander the sands
and wonder
at the miracle of shell and star,
castaway clues to the timeless life that waits
for you beneath the waves,
when you are ready
to discover
yourself.